Pet Chameleons 101 ☺

Keeping & Breeding Healthy Chameleons Made Easy!

Warning and Disclaimer

Every effort has been made to make this digital book as complete and as accurate as possible, but no warranty or fitness is implied. The information provided is on an "as is" basis. The author and the publisher shall have neither liability nor responsibility to any person or entity with respect to any loss or damages arising from the information contained in this digital book.

Table of Contents

In the Accompaning Bonus Reports:

<u>**Bonus 1. Chameleon Journal**</u>

<u>**Bonus 2. Non-Toxic Plant List For Chameleons**</u>

<u>**Bonus 3. Identifying, Treating, and Preventing Medical Problems**</u>

> ➤ Metabolic Bone Disease

> ➤ Thermal Burns

> ➤ Egg Retention

> ➤ Mouthrot (Stomatitis)

> ➤ Hunger Strikes

> ➤ Dehydration

> ➤ Constipation/Impaction

> ➤ Respiratory Infections

> ➤ Tounge Disfunctions

> ➤ Sunken Eyes

Introduction

I love pets but chameleons are my favorite by far. Currently I am the proud owner of Mickey and Doll (both veiled chameleons), Ziggy (a jackson's chameleon), and Doolie (a flapneck chameleon).

This book is designed to prepare potential chameleon owners for their commitment. My goal is to provide information and resources that are capable of answering some of the most asked questions.

On the other hand, this book is not going to discuss the history of chameleons. Nor will it describe each of the varying species. There are a ton of wonderful books out there that discuss these interesting topics. I only want to provide you with resources that you need in order to help your chameleon flourish.

The popularity of chameleons has risen in recent years. In response to this growing market, many enthusiasts are releasing information regarding the health and care of chameleons. Veterinarians have emerged who specialize in reptiles. Supplements have been released that are engineered specifically for chameleons. Even chameleon accessories are becoming popular. Most importantly, there are many organizations that have opened their doors and dedicated themselves to serving the chameleon loving community.

Chameleons might be cute but they should not be taken lightly. Their care requires a substantial amount of effort. They demand 24 hour care so you must plan trips away from home accordingly.

Chapter 1

Getting Started

What Conditions are Required for a Healthy Chameleon?

- An enclosure that is large enough in size.

- Miniature trees for dwelling. They must be the correct depth and width in order to allow for proper thermoregulation.

- Sufficient humidity.

- Water (must be set up so that the reptile can properly utilize it).

- Suitable substrate.

- Logs, sticks, foliage, and other furnishings.

- Gradients that allow for proper heating.

- Correct lighting (must emulate day and night cycles).

- Healthy food.

- Proper disinfecting of the enclosure and all furnishings within.

- Diligent monitoring and all equipment.

- Diligent monitoring of chameleon to catch stress of health issues immediately.

- Access to an experienced veterinarian should trouble arise. Never wait until there is a problem to seek out a veterinarian. Locate one beforehand.

Important Factors to Consider Before Getting your Own Chameleon

This process starts with one very important question. Do you plan to leave for extended periods of time? If yes, then do you have a caretaker who will take care of your chameleon when you are away? Chameleons should not be left unattended. Some owners set up automatic lighting and watering systems so they can leave for a weekend but this is risky. What happens if the power goes out or if a timer malfunctions? Remember that water, lighting, and heating are critical to your chameleon's development and health.

Here are some additional things that you must consider before purchasing a chameleon:

- Are you planning to move? Maybe you're going to University? You must always think ahead before committing to any new pet.

- Are you financially prepared to own a new pet? Chameleons cost more than most people realize since owners have to use specialized veterinarians.

- Can you afford to feed the chameleon?

- Will you have the time to clean out your chameleon's habitat at least twice a week?

- It takes a lot of time to find certain ingredients to provide your feeder insects with the correct nutrients. Are you prepared for this?

- Light fixtures cost quite a bit of money and must be replaced every six months. Are you prepared for this expense?

- Can you afford supplements?

- Are you ready for the responsibility of creating a stimulating environment for your chameleon?

- Do you have any other pets? If you do, then you must ensure that they can never come in contact with your chameleon. Even the mere presence of another pet can stress the chameleon and significantly reduce its lifespan.

- Do you allow smoking in your home? Keep in mind that a chameleon must never be exposed to smoke, air fresheners, or even perfume/cologne.

Where you can Buy a Chameleon

A chameleon's journey to your local pet store involves many different paths. So you should ask your pet store to tell you where it came from. They tend to dress it up by utilizing powerful surroundings that keep your main focus away from the chameleon itself. So examine it carefully.

Do not buy a chameleon from a pet shop that is not willing to tell you where it came from. You have the right and obligation to know. Only deal with reputable pet stores. Stores will normally use a single source to acquire their chameleons: some are good while others are bad.

Professional Breeders

This is the absolute best place to purchase your chameleon. Professional breeders can be found by visiting local showings, contacted through websites, email, or phone, and even deal with large pet store chains.

Adoption

Adopting from a reputable organization is another great option. Many times, reptiles are dropped off at local pet stores by people who are no longer able to commit to their ownership. The reason can vary but generally comes from a hope to make a little money off the pet to trading them in for a more novel pet. My point is that these chameleons have normally been neglected and you will be unaware of complications in their health. One of the most common conditions is MBD (calcium deficiency). Sometimes the manager will try and sell them for upwards of $100! If that's not bad enough, some people will actually try and take them home for breeding purposes! I recommend that you offer to adopt a pet in this condition but never purchase it. The reason is that buying a pet in this condition supports this awful behavior.

Amateur Breeders

Individuals often breed their own chameleons. Sometimes it's done on purpose; sometimes it happens by accident! Generally speaking, amateur breeders have no clue how to properly care for chameleons. Furthermore, they are not conscious of bloodlines. They do it to make a quick buck. Since most pet stores will offer to purchase from anyone, this practice is done a lot more that it probably should be.

Caught in the Wild

Here's a bit of an uncommonly known fact: most chameleons caught in the wild are illegal to own as pets. Some professional breeders do use chameleons caught in the wild to spruce up their blood lines. However, in today's world that not necessary since there is a large enough assortment of captive, tame chameleons to use. Take a moment to imagine the stress that a chameleon must endure when it is captured from the wild and transitioned into captive environment. This should only be attempted by professionals since they must be treated for diseases that can easily spread to other captive chameleons.

Factors to Consider when Buying a Chameleon

The following traits are used to ensure that a chameleon is healthy:

- Are they a good size compared to other hatchlings from the same clutch?

- Chameleons never sleep during the day so their eyes should always be open. Chameleons will rest on branches but they are still alert. If they are closing their eyes during daylight hours then it's a bad sign. They react to light though so if you happen to shut off all lights during the day, they will assume that it's dark. In that instance, they will sleep.

- They should appear plump. This signifies that they are well hydrated and have a healthy appetite.

- A chameleon's color is not a firm indication of its overall health. Their color can change depending on their mood. One exception is a chameleon that is dark or drab. These chameleons could be stressed or cold and this condition can lead to future health concerns.

- Their skin should always be smooth. Chameleons shed their skin very quickly. It's common to see wrinkled skin starting to shed off but be sure that there are no signs of incomplete shedding. This is a sure sign of environmental issues. However, it can also be linked to their metabolic cycle. So just pay attention to them.

- The point on their head should be straight. This is for aesthetic appeal for members of the opposite sex in mating.

- Chameleons should not have lumps on their arms or legs. They should be smooth and straight.

- Chameleons should have good balance.

- Chameleons eat on a daily basis and are constantly interested in food.

- Their feet should have well-formed toes and nails.

- Puffy cheeks, taunt skin, and rounded, raised eyebrows are all signs that a chameleon is hydrated.

Here are some signs that a chameleon is not healthy:

- Lateral folds along the sides of a chameleon's body (or wrinkled skin) is a sign of dehydration.

- Abrasions or cuts.

- Black dots are a sign of mites or ticks.

- Sunken eyes are a bad sign.

- Bumps.

- When a chameleon breathes with its mouth open, they are very likely to be suffering from an upper respiratory infection. Just be sure not to mistake it for behavior that a chameleon is cooling itself down by loosening its jaws and opening its mouth. This is a form of ventilation.

- Misaligned bones.

- Unevenly divided toes or missing nails. Both are signs of inbreeding.

- Bumps along its spine or thick ankles are both signs of MBD.

- Sleeping during the day.

- Lack of coordination.

- Weak grip. Exhibited by an inability to properly grip branches.

Word of Caution!

Never buy a chameleon that is lying down during the day or one that is breathing through its mouth.

Stuff you will Need for your Chameleon

Here is a quick look at some of the basic equipment that you will need to ensure that your chameleon thrives.

Aquarium

The aquarium must be large enough for a full sized chameleon. However, if you are purchasing a hatchling then you will either need to portion off a small section of the tank or purchase an additional, smaller container for temporary use. The goal is to ensure that a hatchling chameleon is not overwhelmed by such a large environment. Remember that when the little fellow is all grown up, he will need a lot of room to move around.

A Large Feeding Bowl

The bowl must be able to hold insects where the hatchling can easily find food. You also need to ensure that insects cannot escape from the bowl. It should be wide, but shallow. Most importantly, it needs to be very slippery so the bugs cannot simply climb up the sides in order to escape. Another helpful tip is to ensure that the bowl is transparent. This allows the chameleon to see the bugs inside from all angles.

Keep in mind that crickets can harm a chameleon! You must provide a constant food source for your pet. If insects are allowed to roam freely, they will start to slowly eat at the flesh of the chameleon. Ouch! Chameleons and crickets should always be kept separately!

Making it easy for your hatchling to find food is the absolute best way to ensure that it stays as healthy as possible. Keep the food bowl in one spot and use a vine as access for your chameleon. Make sure that the vine does not lead directly into the bowl though, lest the insects can simply climb out!

Don't panic if a few insects escape from the bowl. As your chameleon gets older, it may prefer hunting for food rather than eating from the bowl. You must pay close attention. If your chameleon stops eating from the bowl then you should find different ways of feeding it.

By making sure that your feeder insects are kept in a bowl, you are easily able to remove them when you decide to mist. Furthermore, you can remove them individually to feed to your chameleon.

Branches and Foliage

Chameleons require branches in order to thrive and exercise their legs and feet. Branches should be a little larger than a chameleon's feet. This ensures that the animal can walk comfortably.

Sometimes it can be difficult to find branches that are small enough for hatchlings. You'll probably need to take a trip to your local craft store in order to solve this issue. Grapevines and other similar accessories are a great solution to this problem.

Place these branches (or similar accessories) inside of the aquarium or enclosure. Crisscross them to form tiny chameleon highways. Always ensure that accessories are not painted and that they are free from tiny splinters. You can go outside and pick up a few sticks so long as you make sure that they have no small splinters or sharp areas. Bake them at 350 degrees in your oven to disinfect them.

I highly recommend that you use artificial foliage since it's next to impossible to keep real plants free of bacteria. They hold water, which becomes stagnant. Crickets will kick up and disturb real soil. And peralite (found in soil) is toxic to chameleons and they seem to enjoy eating them.

Artificial foliage is much more friendly to an artificial environment because it's versatile. You can use glue to hold them anywhere. Remember that a chameleon loves to dwell in trees so they feel secure.

An Appropriate Substrate

Astroturf is your best bet here. Calcium sand is a close second choice. Anything else can cause serious complications if ingested by a chameleon. Also, be absolutely sure to stay away from wood chips!

Never, ever use newspaper. The humidity will curl up the paper and give insects a hiding place, depriving your chameleon from its meal.

Insects for Feeding

This is not as simple as tossing several bugs into the aquarium and leaving your chameleon to hunting them. You must be careful. For example, a hatchling is not going to be able to capture and eat a large cricket.

Container to Hold Insects

You must have a ventilated container where you can easily provide food for your insects. Use something like empty egg crates so that your insects can hide from each other. They are cannibalistic and will eat one another.

A Watering System

Heavy misting is recommended for hatchlings. Use an eyedropper to offer them water early in their life. The methods used for adult chameleons can be hazardous for hatchings. This includes small ponds.

Lighting Fixtures

You must have UVA/UVB light bulbs for your chameleons. The wattage you need will depend on the size of the aquarium but is normally between 60 and 100. It should be as large as possible so that it covers most of the aquarium.

Appropriate Supplements

This is essential to the healthy development of your chameleon. You will need a calcium and multivitamin.

Humidity and Temperature Gauge

It's important to ensure that your habitat is optimal and the only way to be entirely sure is to gauge temperatures and humidity within the aquarium.

Chapter 2

A Chameleon's Environment

Your Chameleon s Enclosure

First and foremost, always use common sense. The goal is to provide your pet with the closest thing to its natural environment as possible. With that said, let's take a closer look at creating the perfect chameleon enclosure.

Housing a Hatchling

1. Your first goal is to immediately introduce your hatchling to an adult sized aquarium. This must be done as soon as possible. Now the trick is to accessorize only a small portion of this large aquarium so that your hatchling will not venture from this region.

Make it easy for your hatchling to find its food by purchasing a terra-cotta planter and remove the bottom pan. Then simply place all of the food (insects) into the pot. Include a couple of artificial vines that lead into the container so that your chameleon can easily reach its food source. Terra-cotta pots are extremely price friendly and look completely natural so it will not create an eye-sore in your chameleon's aquarium. However, pay close attention to your chameleon. If it does not respond to this food source then you might have to purchase a transparent container to make the insects more visible.

There are numerous advantages to placing food into a separate container but the greatest one is that it prevents the insects from taking refuge under the foliage and ground cover. Another advantage is that it allows you to remove the container before misting the aquarium which prevents the supplements that you have dusted your insects with from simply being washed away. It also gives you the opportunity to remove insects that have not been eaten and reload them, ensuring that they are completely healthy.

Make sure that you do not place your feeder directly under the lamp. The heat from that light will kill them quickly.

If your chameleon is stubborn and does not respond to your feeding method, then you are going to need to change things up. Sometimes you might have to release a couple of insects so that the chameleon will be able to hunt for its prey.

2. Another option for a hatchling is to purchase a small plastic container and placing it inside of the large aquarium. Remove the lid and place the hatchling inside of this container. There are some advantages and disadvantages to this:

Advantages

- It makes the hatchling feel comfortable. A hatchling might feel intimidated by a large aquarium.

- A smaller area makes it much easier for your hatchling to find food.

- The chameleon is in a confined area so you can place insects loosely into the same container (just don't place too many). So this serves as a great method if your chameleon is having problems hunting.

It's essential that you do not allow the insects to bother your chameleon though so place a couple of branches off the ground so that your chameleon can escape the annoyance of the bugs.

Disadvantages

- Chameleons grow at an astonishingly fast rate so it will not like to be confined for long. If you are not careful, you may cause it a great deal of stress.

- A chameleon requires a UVA/UVB light. Placing the pet in a separate container makes it easy to unknowingly create stress by placing the chameleon too far away from it.

- A chameleon can overheat if it doesn't have the room to move around.

Personally, I think that the first method is the best choice since it gives a chameleon the freedom to move around. Plus, most chameleons enjoy hunting bugs. Pay attention to your chameleon and you will be able to determine which method is best.

General Tips

Be careful where you place the aquarium. While it's easy to assume that a chameleon might like the view it will actually annoy the heck it. It will see the tree or plant and try to escape the aquarium in order to climb it. This leads to unnecessary stress. At least three sides of your enclosure should be completely opaque, giving the chameleon some privacy.

You can place the aquarium near a window so long as you pay attention to your chameleon's reaction. If it keeps trying to escape then you should relocate it.

Also, leaving your aquarium near a window can actually kill your chameleon. The sun will shine through the window and cause a greenhouse effect inside of the aquarium. So if you place the container near a window then you should have shades which are close during daylight hours.

Place your enclosure on a desk or table so that it's off of the ground. Chameleons love to dwell in treetops and they love to be high off of the ground. Just be sure not to place it so high that you cannot easily access it.

Avoid your chameleon's reflection. You read that correctly. If a chameleon sees its own reflection then it will mistake it for another chameleon. Since they are a very territorial species, then they will get angry. You can avoid this by applying wallpaper to the aquarium.

Beware of your other pets. For example, cats love to stalk bugs inside of an enclosure and will even jump on top of it. If you do have a cat, then you should keep the chameleon in a separate room and keep the door closed. You should also buy a metal top so that your cat doesn't accidentally fall through it.

Place colored paper along the bottom of the aquarium so that the chameleon can't see through it. It could become stressed if it notices that it cannot get to the ground.

Never grab a chameleon in order to lift it. Their tiny ankles can easily be broken. Instead, gently slide your finger toward it and let it climb onto it.

Remember that your chameleon will react to its environment so it's your job to carefully observe it in order to see any issues that might be causing it undue stress. Never assume that something is not at fault for a reaction simply because it has not reacted in the past to the same object.

Lighting

Lighting is a very important decision that must not be taken too lightly. While there are some money saving options you will need to ensure that they produce a full UVA/UVB spectrum. If it does not produce the full spectrum, then it will negatively affect the metabolic functions of the chameleon. Therefore, your pet will not be able to absorb its vitamins.

Chameleons requires exactly 12 hours of light per day. This allows them to properly produce a vitamin that's critical to properly absorb calcium (Vitamin D3). This light needs to be as close to the chameleon as possible without actually coming into contact with him or any other accessories inside of the aquarium.

Place the light over a branch so that the chameleon will be tempted to bask in its light. It should be placed at a small angle. While water misting will not harm the light, try and avoid spraying any water directly on it for obvious reasons.

Seek out the longest fixture that the enclosure will accommodate. This ensures that your chameleon will get the most out of the lighting. Plus, the bulb itself costs the same for all sizes so you might as well get the largest one possible.

Basking Light

During the summer, you will need to reduce the wattage of your basking light. This is dependant solely on the temperature in the aquarium. Higher watt bulbs can be hazardous, even for large chameleons. Your goal is to create a basking light for your pet, not to heat the entire aquarium.

The inside temperature should be between 65-85 degrees. Furthermore, you must always ensure that the light is at least one foot away from your chameleon. Be sure that your pet cannot climb higher and burn itself on the light. It will attempt to get as close to the light as possible and chameleons do not seem to understand the danger of being burnt.

Basking bulbs are shaped like a mushroom and they have a silver rim. It creates a very specific type of light that is perfect for basking, hence the name. They are designed to only heat a select area. Make sure that you stay away from those clear blue bulbs that are on the market. These tend to produce too much heat.

Don't allow yourself to be convinced to buy a bulb simply because it's cheaper. Sure, it might save you some money in the moment but will burn out quickly. If that's not bad enough, they do not produce a quality basking zone.

Make sure that you keep a spare bulb on hand at all times. They can go out at any given moment and you do not want your chameleon to be left in the dark. While it's possible to use a normal light bulb for an emergency, it's not recommended since they distribute heat throughout the entire aquarium and not just a small area.

I recommend that you invest in a dome style fixture since this style can be placed flush atop of the enclosure. It should remain at least one foot away from your chameleon and any materials inside of the tank. Furthermore, you can also buy a suspension device that will allow you to adjust the height of your lamp. This device will also make the fixture more safe by ensuring that other pets and children do not knock it over. Heck, even a chameleon can go rogue and knock over an unsecured lamp.

Thermal burns are the number one cause of death of chameleons in captivity.

Only use nocturnal bulbs as a heat source if the temperature inside of a room drops below 65 degrees – which is not likely to happen indoors. Your chameleon must have a period to cool down. Day/Night cycles happen naturally so they must be recreated within an artificial environment. Living in a habitat that is constantly being heated will mess up the chameleon's metabolism, causing them to be unhappy and not want to eat.

Bulbs should be replaced every six months since their ability to create a true spectrum will diminish over time.

Additional Information

It's extremely important to ensure that your chameleon has a bashing spot on one side of the aquarium that is around 90 – 105 degrees while ensuring that the rest of the area is cooler. In fact, the whole aquarium should be around 70 at night and 80 during the day. Some breeds of chameleons that are not given adequate areas to bask will develop respiratory issues.

The wattage required for a bulb to generate an appropriately heated basking spot will very as the ambient temperature changes. Never try and guess what the temperature is. Install a thermometer inside of the aquarium so you are not forced to guess. Slightly raise the wattage until you reach the desired temperature. Also remember that different types of bulbs will produce different temperatures.

Accessories

I recommend that you use artificial vines and flowers for climbing surfaces but stay away from berries or beads that might look like water droplets. The chameleon might try and ingest them! You can use real plants to improve the quality of air inside of the habitat and copy its natural environment. Just don't use real plants for vines and pay close attention to the soil – most importantly, those tiny white beads that form in soil. They are toxic to chameleons and they will actually eat them! Never allow this to happen. Furthermore, if you do decide to use real plants then you should circulate them with fake ones. For example, use real plants one month and fake plants the next month. The reason is that the water in plants can breed bacteria. In fact, it might be a better idea to use fake plants and install an air circulation system into the aquarium in order to avoid problems while still ensuring the freshness of the air.

If you choose to use real branches then you should harvest them yourself. Get them during the winter so they are easier to clean. Use sand paper to make them smooth and remove small splinters. Just be sure they are not so smooth that your chameleon cannot climb on them!

Then soak them in detergent, scrubbing with a wire brush to ensure that they are free of harmful bacteria.

Please have a look at the bonus report "Non-Toxic Plant List" for a list of suitable (non-toxic) plants that can be used in a chameleon's enclosure.

A bird ladder is also a great addition to a chameleon's environment. They are quite inexpensive and can be found in the bird section of any pet supply store.

If you plan to buy a plant to add to the aquarium, ensure that it has not been treated with any harmful pesticides. You don't want your chameleon exposed to these harmful chemicals.

A veggie-clip also makes a great addition to your habitat and they can be found in the reptile section of a pet store. This is basically a plastic cup that is attached to a suction cup. You place it on the cool side of the aquarium and place lettuce inside. This allows your chameleon to munch on some delicious veggies!

Things that you view as purely aesthetic might be seen by your chameleon as functional. Make sure that sticks and vines used for climbing are strongly secured. You can use glue to stick artificial foliage to the walls of the aquarium. Since the glue is easy to peel off, you can change things up from time-to-time. Try creating fun bridges for your chameleon.

Be sure you don't use any glue while your chameleon is inside of the aquarium. Wait at least 20 minutes to ensure that the vapors have dissipated before letting your pet return home. Clean up all excess glue so that your pet does not ingest it.

Glue should be used very sparingly. It's a great way to adapt the environment but only if you follow this one simple rule. Clean it up and ensure that no dry glue is within reach of the chameleon. It will find it and it will try to eat it.

Keep it as simple as possible. Elaborate obstacles will cause you to procrastinate cleaning the tank.

There are only three choices for substrate that are safe for chameleons: astro turf, calcium sand, and none at all. Never use towels or newspapers since insects can hide under it. While wood chips might increase the humidity, there is a chance that your chameleon might ingest them while hunting. This can lead to serious (and fatal) health concerns. Substrate is not a requirement since chameleons prefer to stay above the ground anyway. However, during the colder parts of the year you may consider adding substrate for insulation purposes.

Do not place branches too close to the basking light since chameleons will be drawn to the heat. You can see the signs of thermal burn if you pay attention. The first sign is a light, green patch of skin. It will gradually turn black. Afterwards, small blisters will start to form on the chameleon. Since they do not seem too worried about being burnt, you must do the worrying for them! Thermal burn is the leading cause of death of chameleons.

How to Clean your Chameleon's Enclosure

I recommend that you use bleach diluted with water to clean the enclosure. Start off by removing everything from the tank and then use a sponge to wipe saturate the entire aquarium. Then you should use a scouring pad to scrub the entire area. You will find that some areas have accumulated sediments that must be wiped away. Hot water and bleach will help to dissolve them. Even glue can be removed using this strategy.

Once you have thoroughly sterilized the enclosure, you must make absolutely sure that all of the bleach is rinsed out. This can easily be accomplished with a clean sponge and bucket filled with clean water. Use clean water to rinse out the aquarium and then sponge up that water. Repeat until you are absolutely sure that there is no bleach left. Use your misting bottle to remove any debris from small corners that might be difficult to reach normally. Remember that when you are using any cleaning products that they can harm your pet if not rinsed out. So be careful.

For cleaning the foliage inside of the tank, you should let them soak in a bathtub and let them soak in a bleach solution. Then drain out that bleach and use fresh water to get off the harmful bleach. Rinsing is extremely important.

You should also clean the branches that your chameleon uses to climb. You can do this by simply using a scoring pad and rubbing them with soapy water.

When using a bowl or watering system with an air pump then you will need to replace the water on a daily basis. The bowl should be cleaned at least once a week. Use the same method that you would for cleaning the tank. Chameleons prefer to pee in water. Insects will also fall into the water and die. Your job is to ensure that your chameleon always has safe, fresh water delivered to it.

Rope that are made from fabric should be avoided since they can't be cleaned good enough to ensure safety.

Finally, if you notice any stains on the glass of the aquarium then use CLR to remove these deposits.

Chapter 3

Watering your Chameleon

General Information and Tips

You can find rubber eyedroppers in the reptile department of your local pet shop. Even if you have gotten your chameleon used to drinking from a rubber eyedropper, he will still feel the irresistible urge to lick water from leaves.

You should also ensure that your chameleon gets water that is room temperature. We might love cold water but put yourself in the position of your chameleon. Would you be drinking cold water in your natural environment if you were a chameleon? The answer is no. So you should ensure that your pet gets water that is close to its natural environment. Experts recommend that you give it only bottled water but you can also boil your own.

Chameleons can absorb small amounts of water through their skin so you must spray their environment at least two times every day. Use warm water to increase the humidity (chameleons love humidity). Don't be afraid to use hot water since it will cool down once infused into the air.

Pay attention to the force you are spraying your water since it's possible to use too much force. Focus the water on leaves and the walls of the habitat.

Make sure that you move your basking lamp when you are misting your chameleon's habitat. The water can rise and contact the bulb, causing it to explode. Of course, this will be harmful to the little fellow that's minding his own business perched on his favorite branch.

Don't let puddles of water accumulate in the aquarium. It will contaminate the environment because insects will fall into these puddles and die.

Clean its eyes by spraying the chameleon gently.

Setting up a Great Watering System

Your chameleon will need fresh water on a daily basis. Kind of obvious, right? Well I see so many owners wait until water looks murky before they change it. Your chameleon might drink all of the time or maybe you will never see it drink. But I can assure you that it is drinking. You should change the water every day to ensure that it's getting only fresh water. There are two methods of watering your chameleon so you should never limit it to just a single method.

Using an Eyedropper

You can purchase an eyedropper from any pet store; just check out the reptile section. Many chameleons will openly accept an eyedropper while others might not understand it at first. If the latter is true then you will need to keep trying until they learn. Here's how:

• Start off by holding the dropper a few inches from the chameleon's face and let drops fall on its lips. This will allow it to see and feel the droplets.

The only downside to this method is that someone must be there to hold the dropper. So it will only work so long as you are there to offer your chameleon a drink. Never use glass droppers since your pet can bite down and hurt himself.

Show your chameleon that the dropper has water in it by slowly letting it drip where they can see it. The droplets will attract the reptile. Once you get a response, then allow a drop to touch its nose. It can take some time before your pet gets the hang of it so be persistent.

Another awesome trick is to spray then with a light mist of water. He will open his mouth to lick the moisture in the air. When he does, let a small bit of water drop into its mouth. Don't try to force water into his mouth. Chameleons drink by tapping their tongue on the water. They do not gulp it. Once they understand that the dropper is water, they will move toward it. Pay attention to the reaction of your chameleon. If its head is tilted toward the ceiling, he is attempting to drain the water. Allow him to do so before giving him more water.

The Ice Cube Method

Some individuals choose to use another method of delivering water to the chameleons. They place ice cubes atop the aquarium so that the water will drip down. The chameleon can then drink it. The only downside is that it's not constant since the ice cubes will melt away. Another way of using ice cubes is to fill a large, plastic cup with ice cubes. Then punch a small hole in the bottom of the cup so that the water drips slowly into the tank as the ice melts. Just remember to place a small container inside of the aquarium that will catch the water.

When using the ice cube method, be sure that there is at least one branch close to the dropping water. It should be close enough for your chameleon to reach them. Do this while also ensuring that it does not get too close to the backing light. Finally, add a few rocks to the container inside of the tank. That ensures that your chameleon cannot fall in and drown.

The Spritzing Method

Small droplets of water glistening in the light attract chameleons. When you are misting the inside of your chameleon's habitat, be sure that some droplets form on objects inside of the aquarium. Even if your chameleon is drinking normally you should still do this since it allows the reptile to follow its instincts. It loves to lick these droplets!

The Pond Method

You have two options here: you can either place a shallow bowl in your aquarium or you can purchase a reptile hammock from your local pet store that hangs in the corner. Whatever of these you choose, you should also invest in a small air pump to create bubbles in the water. This will attract most chameleons.

It's essential that you never use this method for hatchlings since it creates a significant risk of drowning. You should place rocks inside to ensure that your chameleon can get out if it accidentally falls in.

Water bowls must be sterilized at least once a week and you should replace the water on a daily basis. Chameleons urinate in water and insects fall in and die so you'll have to keep this water source clean.

Advantages of Using The Pond Method

- Chameleons absolutely love to drink from ponds if there are bubbles in it! However, without these bubbles a chameleon will ignore it.

- Ponds look awesome in a chameleon's environment.

Disadvantages of Using The Pond Method

- A pond can be quite unhealthy if it's not cleaned on a regular basis.

- It can be difficult to change water if the pond is connected to a hammock, which is extremely popular among chameleon owners.

- The water source gets contaminated easily since chameleons will urinate in it and bugs will fall in and drown.

- A small air pump is noisy and the pump must be cleaned thoroughly on a monthly basis or it will get clogged.

- There is always the risk of your chameleon drowning. You can limit this risk by placing rocks inside of the pond but you can never eliminate it altogether.

Showering a Chameleon

If you are following the advice in this book then your chameleon should be healthy and well hydrated. Now I am going to discuss showers for a moment since many people love steaming their chameleon. If you decide that you want to try this, follow one of the following methods. Just be sure that the water/steam does not get too hot or it could actually dehydrate your chameleon.

Chameleons are quite delicate and even 30 minutes in a hot bathroom can be unhealthy. However, this is a very useful way of helping a chameleon that is having issues defecating. If you notice this symptom in your chameleon then there is likely an underlying problem causing it. This can be impaction, incorrect humidity, temperature, or even some bad food at one point. Showering can actually help to clear it up.

What you Should <u>Never</u> Do:

- First and foremost, never put a chameleon directly into a shower. The water pressure is just too high.

- Do not place a chameleon into a bathtub that has water in it – even if it's a small amount. Chameleons drown very easily and will become very stressed if they are exposed to something that is not natural to them.

- Never expose a chameleon to bath oil, soap, or even shampoo.

What you Should Do:

- Buy a cotton rope and hang it from your shower head so that your chameleon can hang out with you while you shower or bathe. Just be sure that you don't accidentally get shampoo on them. Also, never leave them alone. They might accidentally fall into the tub!

- Put a small amount of warm water in the sink and bathe your chameleon. Use a baster to gently pour water over him. Replace it frequently with more warm water.

- If your chameleon is sick or dehydrated, then soak him twice a day in baby safe fluid which is found in the baby section of your drug store.

• You can also place a large plant on the bathroom floor and let your chameleon hang out there while you shower.

Chapter 4

What to Feed Your Chameleon

Offer a Variety

Variety is the key to a healthy chameleon. They love to have both vegetation and insects to munch on. This promotes a healthy appetite. Chameleons are easily bored so if you try and feed them the same bugs every day, then they will stop eating. Therefore, it's critical that you mix up their diet and offer up different types of insects.

Offer your chameleon food around three times a week to keep him interested. Again, chameleons get bored very easily so if you feed him every day then he might stop eating. This is only true for adults; hatchlings will need a constant supply.

Here are some insects that you can feed your chameleon:

Crickets: The most common food for chameleons are crickets. Plus crickets are also easy to gut feed.

Grasshoppers: Grasshoppers are another common food choice for chameleons. They also offer more nutritional value than crickets. However, the downside is that grasshoppers are often difficult to find.

Flies: Chameleons often eat these in the wild so they deserve a mention here. As you might have guessed though, they are difficult for captive chameleons to catch. You're probably better off visiting the fish section of your local pet shop and buying dried flies.

Hornworms: The two different types of hornworms are named respectively after the plants they consume. You can purchase and grow them. Hornworms will eventually become hawk moths. Some owners choose to allow this transformation to occur and then release the moth into their chameleon's habitat.

Silkworms: This is a highly recommended addition to a chameleon's diet. You can buy them as eggs and raise these worms yourself. Once they get nice and large, feed them to your chameleon. Silkworms will also transform into moths.

Waxworms: Most pet shops sell waxworms since they can be fed to many different types of pets. It's worth noting that waxworms do not offer nutritional value to your chameleon. Think of them like a treat.

Mealworms: These worms will eventually transform into beetles. Larger versions of this worm can bite you so be extra careful when handling them. This worm can be gut fed to provide even more nutritional value to your lizard.

Cockroaches: Cockroaches are easy to purchase since most pet shops stock them. Try and find the specimen of cockroach that cannot climb glass walls. They breed quickly so you can farm an endless supply for your lizard. Finally, they easy to gut load.

Tips

- Any insects that you offer your chameleon must be bred specifically for food. Insects that you might find outside have a high chance of being exposed to pesticides that will poison your chameleon!

- Always gut-load insects for at least 24 hours before feeding them to your chameleon. Pet stores do not gut-load insects so that task will fall on you.

- Never feed dead insects to your chameleon. Furthermore, don't feed them any insects that have escapes and are wandering around your home. Unhealthy crickets appear a much darker color than normal.

- Only feed insects small amounts of food at a time. Offering up large amounts of food at once will only lead to molding and rotting food. This food can actually contaminate your chameleon if they consume an insect that has eaten moldy food. Remove uneaten food daily and spread it out so that it takes longer to mold.

Bringing Feeder Insects Home

When you purchase feeder insects, the store will place the bugs in a container of some kind. This is usually a clear, plastic bag. It's important that you place them into an appropriate container as soon as possible. Egg crates are best reserved for crickets since they must be kept separate or they will eat each other. Worms are kept in woodchips, oatmeal, or anything else they can burrow under.

Store your insects at room temperature. Never leave them in your vehicle. They can die very quickly. The best thing to do is to bring your own container and ask the store to put them directly into your containers. That way you are already prepared and they will experience very little shock.

Once you are home, transfer crickets into a special critter container which you can find at any pet store. This container is clear and comes equipped with a removable lid. Do not try and save money by making this container yourself. It will not be the correct size. Crickets must have space or they will die from one of the following things:

- Being smothered

- Starvation or dehydration because they cannot find food/water

- Being eaten by other crickets

Pour the bag of crickets directly into the container and then place egg cartons into the same container. After which you should gut-load them for at least 24 hours before feeding them to your chameleon.

How to Gut-Load your Feeder Insects

Gut-loading is the process of feeding your insects certain foods before feeding them to your chameleon. Many of the insects you buy are suffering from dehydration and malnutrition. You know the saying "you are what you eat?" Well your chameleon is what it eats too! They will not get the proper nourishment from an insect suffering from dehydration and malnutrition. You will need to feed your insects a specialized menu if you want them as nutritious as possible for your pet.

Quick Schedule for Gut-Loading your Insects

1st Week: Collard greens, tropical fish food flakes, and oranges.

2nd Week: Melon, crushed dry iguana diet, mustard greens.

3rd Week: Carrots, crushed alfalfa pellets, crushed high quality cat food.

Many people fall prey to the myth that insects are tough as nails. They are actually extremely delicate and will die within hours if the conditions are not perfect. Not only is this quite costly; it's unsanitary.

Guidelines

- Certain insects can coexist. One example is that crickets and superworms can be stored in the same container. However, waxworms must be kept separate since they will be eaten by other insects.

- Although I did use mixing superworms and crickets in an example above, I recommend that you keep them separate since they burrow. They can be difficult to collect when stored with crickets. In fact, crickets might escape while you are trying to find your superworms!

- Any deep container works for storing worms. You do not even need a lid since they cannot get out. However, if you have another pet roaming the house then you should probably use a lid since that pet might get curious and tip the works over!

- Make sure that you save up enough egg crates before you buy crickets. Ask the shop where you make the purchase if they have any bedding for worms. You can also use plain oatmeal for worms.

Other Food Items

One common sense rule with feeding is that you should never feed your insects anything that is not healthy for your chameleon. With that said, here is a quick look at some of the food items that are safe to feed your chameleon.

Dry Foods

- Crushed alfalfa blacks from local feed store

- Dried sea kelp

- Oatmeal

- Wheat germ

- Bee pollen

- Monkey chow

- Raw, unsalted sunflower seeds

- Baby Parrot food

- Rice baby cereal, Gerber or Beechnut

- Dried sea kelp

- Dried egg yolk

Vegetation

- Bok Choy

- Mustard greens Carrots

- Sweet Potato

- Collard greens

- Dandelion leaves

- Romaine lettuce Escarole

- Kale

- Squash

Fruit

- All citrus fruits

- Prickly pear cactus

- Blueberries

- Apples/peaches (not the seeds!)

- Mango

Food Tips

- Always research a food before feeding it to your chameleon. Never trust anyone without verifying it. Foods like apricots, peaches, and spinach might seem like a good food source but they actually have portions that are toxic to chameleons!

- Most grocery stores have a discounted section for older products. You can find great deals on foods to feed your chameleons and insects.

- A chameleon will not eat a whole piece of fruit since they cannot chew food. Instead, you will need to either crush it or feed them baby food.

- Under no circumstances should you ever feed canned fruit to a chameleon. The added sugar is not healthy to them.

More About Baby Food

If your chameleon gets sick then you can feed him some baby food. This also goes for a rebellious reptile that's decided to go on a hunger strike. Just be sure not to try and force feed an animal unless it's absolutely necessary. Also, don't become dependant on feeding your pet baby food since it's not the healthiest choice for chameleons. Furthermore, feeding your chameleon too much might make it lazy so it stops hunting on its own. As you can see, it's only recommended to use baby food in an absolute emergency.

Some vets will actually recommend a special kind of cat food over baby food. High proteins found in cat food make this a great alternative.

You can actually add extra protein to baby food by adding dry flies to it. These can be purchased in the fish section of a pet store.

Supplementation

Supplementation	Brand	Frequency
Calcium (no phosphorous)	Repti-Cal	Every feeding
Multivitamin	VIOLITE by Tera	1-2 times a week.
Two in One (Calcium and vitamins!)	MINER-ALL by Sticky Tongue Farms*	Babes to half-grown daily. Half-grown to sub-adults every 2nd feeding. Adults every 3rd feeding

*Sticky Tongue s Miner-All can be difficult to find. Ask your pet store to order it!

Note: Remember, too much or too little calcium/multivitamins can harm your chameleon!

Chapter 5

General Care

Things you Should Never Do

You should not allow two chameleons to occupy the same habitat – even if they seem to get along. Over time, they will become stressed. That stress will cause them to attack each other, causing injury or possible death.

As I mentioned earlier, you should always ensure that your basking lamp is at least one foot away from reach of your chameleon. At the same time, don't keep it too far away. The closer the better. I recommend that you keep it 15 inches from the closest branch.

Don't overload your chameleon's habitat with too much foliage. Chameleons will definitely need places to hide but they also love space. On that note, you should not place rocks inside of the habitat either. Reptiles have the weird trait of not recognizing when they are being burned so they will climb up on a hot rock and not notice themselves being slowly baked! Even if a chameleon gets burnt, it will not learn from the experience. It will climb back on the same rock and get burnt again.

Never keep the entire aquarium the same temperature. Chameleons require both a warm and cool zone. Keeping them hot all of the time will lead to dehydration and eventually, death.

Do not leave your chameleon outside without supervision. This might seem like common sense, but some owners make the mistake of thinking that a quick bathroom break will be fine. They are only gone a minute and return only to find that their chameleon has ran off. They are extremely quick and agile. It can get up a tree or hide under a brush very quickly. By the time you start looking in one place, it will have already moved to another. There is almost zero chance of finding a chameleon outdoors. If you must take your chameleon outside, then always keep your eye on it.

In fact, I don't recommend you taking your chameleon outside since there are so many risks. Not only can it get lost, but birds love to swoop down and claim them. Plus there might be pesticides on the ground. It's just not worth the risk.

Although I don't really recommend you to travel with your chameleon, if you absolutely must then take some precautions:

- Take a small container and eye dropper with you

- Carry a spray bottle

- Purchase a large travel container

- Constantly provide you chameleon with water

- Carry all essential housing equipment with you

Never leave a chameleon unattended for long periods of time. For example, you must be home before it cools down to ensure that the temperature inside of the habitat does not drop below 65 degrees.

If you want to let your chameleon enjoy the summer then you can invest in a bird cage (one designed for small birds). This is actually a cheap method and has the added advantage of being easy to transport. Just be sure not to place it on the ground. Remember that chameleons prefer to be above the ground. Also, be sure to keep it out of the reach of other pets or critters.

You will need to be absolutely sure that your chameleon cannot squeeze out of the cage. You might be surprised at how small of a space a chameleon can squeeze through. They will climb around the perimeter of the cage, searching for a way out so you must be absolutely sure that there are no tears of gaps.

If you are allowing your chameleon to enjoy the outdoors (in their cage) then never leave it unsupervised. You might think the weather is perfect and that you're not hurting it. Remember that they cannot regulate their own body temperature. Chameleons depend on their environment to do it for them. As the day progresses, a chameleon will either get too hot or too cold. You must move the cage around in order to find the ideal conditions. It only takes an hour for a chameleon to die from overexposure to be responsible!

Do not pull your chameleon off of a branch – ever! They have very fragile bones and you could break its leg. I know that it can become frustrating when you need to get your pet off of a rope of stick when you decide to clean but do not allow this frustration to fuel you. Instead, glide your fingers gently under his feet slowly. He will need his feet on solid ground (or your finger) before letting do.

Constructing your Outdoor Enclosure

Outdoor enclosures can be tricky business. You can use leaves from surrounding trees if you like, just avoid the toxic plants. It is also okay to use non-sterile branches for your outdoor enclosure but you must be sure to check them for bugs, splinters, or other hazards. Never bring those branches inside though. Also, you must change them daily since the heat and moisture can allow bacteria to thrive inside of these branches.

Ensure that there is a shaded area inside of the enclosure so that your reptile has a place to cool down. There should also be a basking area for it to warm up in but that should be fairly easy to find outdoors in the summer.

Do not keep your chameleon in a high traffic area where there is a lot of activity. They love privacy. The stress of a high traffic zone will shorten its life a lot.

While you can most certainly place your reptile in a window for the view, you must ensure that no sunbeams come through and impact the aquarium. It might not seem like a big deal to the naked eye, but remember that the enclosure will create a greenhouse effect. And remember that it only takes an hour for a chameleon to die from overexposure.

If you notice that your reptile is at the bottom of the tank moving around and trying to get out, then there could be something wrong. At this point you will need to start paying close attention. Check the temperature gauges to ensure that the temperature is within tolerance. If the chameleon keeps acting in this manner, this something might be irritating it. Actually, if you have a female then she could be looking for a place to lay her eggs!

Avoid placing your chameleon in view of another or even their own reflection. It will cause them a lot of stress.

Don't attempt to get a chameleon to change colors on queue. This causes stress.

Do not allow more than one person at a time to view your chameleon. They are extremely shy and solitary. Only allow one person at a time to view it.

Female Chameleons

One of the most asked question I hear is "How can I tell a male and female chameleon apart?"

Let me answer that question. Male chameleons have bumps decorating the backs of their heels. The scientific term for these are tarsal spurs. As males age, they are usually noticeably larger than females, have taller casques, and much more prominent gullar crests. Of course, this all depends on the season, age, and mood of the chameleon.

Females tend to lay infertile eggs several times a year so you will need to be prepared for this. Why? Because she will stop eating and then she will start crawling around on the ground, scratching at the sides of the enclosure. When you notice these signs then you should move your chameleon to another enclosure with sandbox style sand. Just ensure that it's moist enough to dig and not collapse inward. This sand should be around a foot and a half deep.

Female chameleons love to dig a deep hole and then sit to lay their eggs. If the sand is not deep or moist enough, then she will not lay them. Here are some additional tips to keep in mind:

- It's important that you do not offer her food while in the sandy container. The insects will just bother her and she isn't in the mood to eat anyway.

- Ensure that she has heat and UVA/UVB bulbs to bask in. Just be sure that it's not too close! In fact, you might consider using a lower wattage.

- Mist her with water so long as you are not disturbing her.

- Stay away since she will need privacy to lay her eggs.

When night comes, I recommend that you place her back into her normal habitat. It's not a good idea to let a chameleon sleep on moist sand because it will cool down at night. Once you move the chameleon back to its normal habitat, you can then check the sand to see if there are any eggs. If you don't find any eggs, then repeat the same process for a couple of days. Remember to offer her water during this process and to feed her liquid calcium on a daily basis.

If you gently rub your chameleon's belly, you can easily feel the presence of eggs. If she does not lay them within a few days then you might need to take a trip to the vet. They have drugs that can help her to contract. Then if that still doesn't work, they will have to remove them with surgery.

Female chameleons can reach maturity within three months!

Some Final Notes

While your female is laying eggs, you will need to make absolutely sure that you give it water and calcium – you must do this manually. The eggs absorb most of the nutrients that are ingested by the chameleon. So your chameleon becomes weakened.

If your chameleon doesn't lay her eggs within a certain amount of time then they will continue to develop and eventually suffocate her by compressing her lungs. However, if you do not ensure that she is getting enough calcium then she will become too weak to lay the eggs. Furthermore, nutrition intake important even after the egg laying process is finished.

If you choose to purchase a female chameleon, then you will have to be even more observant than normal. Once you notice the symptoms mentioned above, you only have a few days to ensure that she lays her eggs. If she does not, then she must be taken to a vet immediately.

Chapter 6

FAQ & Top Tips

Frequently Asked Questions

Here are some of the most common question asked by chameleon owners.

Q: How much is a chameleon supposed to drink?

A: First of all, you should replace your chameleon's water daily so that it's fresh. Some owners rarely see their chameleon drinking. There are other methods of giving water to your reptile though. See the previous section on hydration.

Q: How much is a chameleon supposed to eat?

A: Hatchings have huge appetites and can eat up to 30 bugs a day so you should be sure that they have a steady supply of food. Although it's possible for them to overeat, it's extremely rare. In most cases they will just nibble all day. Keep a large amount in the feeder bowl to the it's easy for them to find food. What I like to do is place a wide, deep bowl at the bottom of the habitat. Then I use my glue gun to add a few trigs that lead down into the bow. This gives my chameleon easy access.

Furthermore, it's critical that your chameleon be given calcium supplements from day one. As it matures, it will need the calcium to strengthen its bones. Its rapid growth can lead to a weak structure that is not able to hold up its weight.

Q: Can more that one chameleon be kept in the same habitat?

A: NO! Chameleons are a very territorial species and will become irritated if they are in the same habitat as another chameleon. This will lead to a lot of stress. Also, it's not uncommon for chameleons to eat one another!

Q: Do I need to make sure that my chameleon gets shots? Does it need to be spayed or neutered?

A: Chameleone don't need shots like other pets and since you are not going to be housing them together, you do not have to neuter males. However, you should consider having your female spayed since she will lay eggs regardless of whether or not they are fertilized. In other words, she does not need to mate in order to lay eggs. If conditions are not ideal then she will retain those eggs and eventually die.

Q: Do Chameleons like to be pet?

A: Actually, they do! Under the chin is a great spot to pet your chameleon.

Q: Will my chameleon recognize me?

A: Absolutely!

Q: Do chameleons eat vegetation?

A: Most of them will not eat vegetation so if yours is not munching on greenery, that's actually a great sign. Chameleons normally eat vegetation in order to get water.

Q: How will I know if my chameleon is sick?

A: Most chameleons will keep drinking and eating when they are sick so it's difficult to notice when one has a serious illness. There are blood tests that can be done but they are quite stressful to the animal. I recommend that you take a photograph of the reptile once a month and use them as a reference to detect changes.

More Tips

A chameleon's shedding cycle is one of the best indicators of health. It can also reflect certain environmental variables like heat and humidity.

Chameleons will go on hunger strikes that are triggered by several different variables like seasonal changes or boredom from their current diet. When a chameleon goes on one of these hunger strikes it is not an automatic sign that something is seriously wrong. Here are a few quick tips for when your chameleon goes on a hunger strike:

- You should always start off by offering your chameleon different insects that those it has been eating.

- Keep the blinds closed during the winter.

- Put all of the lights on timers to simulate night/day cycles.

If a chameleon starts wandering around the bottom of its habitat then something might be wrong. It usually means that the chameleon is looking for cooler place to rest. So you will need to ensure that you provide your chameleon with a cool area.

Never attempt to fix problems with those so-called remedies that you might find at a local store. Make an appointment with your vet and have your reptile checked out by a specialist. There is a huge difference between treating symptoms and treating the problem.

Finally, a sure sign of your chameleon being sick is when it sits with its eyes closed all day and/or breathes through its mouth.

Fast Facts

Veiled Chameleons are classified as the following:

Family: Chamelonidae

Species: Calyptratus (veiled)

- Chameleon means "Little Lion" when translated.

- An individual who studies reptiles is called a Herpetologist.

- The care for reptiles is known as husbandry.

- Chameleons are not the only animal capable of changing their color. There are species of fish, frogs, and other lizards who also share this ability.

- Chameleons have a pigment called Melanin located in various cells in their skin. This pigment is what gives it the ability to change color.

- The reason a chameleon's skin normally appears green is because the yellow and blue pigments are the ones that can normally be seen. When the dark melanin spreads, the chameleon becomes darker. When other colors spread, they mix with the narural yellow and blue.

- Chameleons are classified as ectotherms. An ectotherm is an animal whose body temperature is regulated by their environment.

- A chameleon will react to the temperature by changing color, just as it does the physical environment. They are dependant on the temperature around them to heat and cool them. Thus, their environment helps them move, hunt, and even digest food. When basking, you might notice your chameleon turns half-black and half-green. This is done purposely since black is the best color in the spectrum at absorbing heat.

- Chameleons can even communicate merely by changing colors! If they feel threatened then their emotions will cause them to turn a specific color.

- A chameleon cannot protect itself by merely changing color to match its environment. It also walks a certain way to emulate surrounding objects. For example, it may sway back and forth while walking in order to imitate a leaf blowing in the wind.

- Chameleons will eat their own dead skin once it has shed off!

- Chameleons have taste buds.

- Chameleons can smell but their sense of smell is very limited.

- A Chameleon's ears are not visible with the naked eye. Their sense of hearing tends to lean towards hearing vibrations in the air. This helps them to stay safe and hunt.

- Chameleons do have teeth that are used to help them kill prey. However, they might swallow a bug whole or swallow it. They seem to have mixed feeling about this. Furthermore, sometimes a chameleon will hold food in its mouth for several minutes before chewing/swallowing it.

- A chameleon will throw up if it eats something that it does not like or if it's sick. This can be unhealthy since it dehydrates the chameleon.

- Male chameleons have Tarsal Spurs on the backs of their heels. These are small nubs. Furthermore, they develop larger casques than females.

- A Chameleon's vision is Binocular which means that each of their eyes operate independently. They see like humans do. This is much different than other reptiles that can see one image with each eye.

- A chameleon's tail is prehensile, just like a monkey. They can use it to grip objects!

- A veiled chameleon's toes are group opposite of each other. This is known as Zygodactyl feet.

- Contrary to popular belief, chameleons cannot re-grow their tails. Most other reptiles can, but chameleons are the exception.

- Chameleons are arboreal, meaning they prefer to dwell off of the ground. They are rarely seen walking on the ground so when they do then something is generally wrong. There are two exceptions: one is when a female is looking to lay her eggs and the other is when they are hunting. However, some rare species of chameleons live their entire life on the ground.

- Chameleons can see in color! This is contrary to most reptiles.

- Chameleons are climbers. Their hands and feet are built perfectly for gripping branches. They do not like surfaces with no traction.

- Chameleons like to sleep upside down or in a corner so if you notice yours doing this, don't panic. It's perfectly normal.

- Chameleons much shed their skin since it does not expand as they grow.

- A chameleon does not shed all of its skin at once. It can shed it in patches and it can take weeks. Hatchlings tend to shed once every few weeks since they grow quickly but once it becomes an adult, that rate will slow to around every 4 months.

- A chameleon will puff up when it's ready to shed. You'll notice it rubbing against rocks, twisting about, and even trying to use its feet to pull off the dead skin. It probably itches like crazy!

- Don't help pick or pull at the dead skin. It will fall off naturally. You might harm your chameleon if you try and help pull off the dead skin. The underlying skin is likely too sensitive to pull off if it has not done so.

- Chameleons are extremely territorial and are not a sociable pet. They will even feel threatened by their own reflection!

- Chameleons have issues with depth perception. A hatching might take off running without any warning. It can even run right out of your hands. Beware of this since it can quickly find a place to hide.

- A chameleon's shed cycle is a great way to determine its health. Keep a journal to log when it sheds. You should also log any other unusual behavior.

- If a chameleon is sleeping during the day then that is a sure sign that it's sick. This is not natural.

Chapter 7

Chameleon Breeds

Panther Chameleon

This chameleon is characterized by vibrant colors so it's often considered one of the most aesthetically pleasing breed. In fact, some people even consider it to be the most eye-catching lizard in the entire animal kingdom. Males can be around 20 inches in size while females are a bit smaller. In addition to its size, male Panther Chameleons are identified by their vivid color in comparison to females. Females will also lose their color when laying eggs to show males that she is not interested in mating. Panther chameleons live for an average of 10 years but females will only live two to three years after laying eggs.

Fischer's Chameleon

This breed of chameleon possesses a very distinct difference between males and females, making it easy to identify its gender. Males are much larger and have a distinguishable horn that extends from their forehead. Females are much smaller but contrary to popular belief, they also have horns. However, a female's horn is only about an eighth of the size of the males. Fischer chameleons are tough and thrive in high temperatures and humidity.

High Casqued Chameleon

High Casqued chameleons can be found in a variety of different colors. It often displays a dark color when basking since these darker colors offer optimum light absorption. Like most breeds, males are noticeably larger than females. Males have a single horn extending from thier forehead, a serrated back, and tiny spikes that run along their neck. Females do not share any of these features.

Males will express their desire to mate by sporting brilliant colors in an effort to compete with other males. High Casqued chameleons can also extend their tongues to the same length as their body!

Jackson's Chameleon

The Jackson's chameleon only grows to around 12 inches and has a varying lifespan. It will reach its sexual maturity at around the five month point. Although most Jackson's chameleons are bright green, there are instances where blue and even yellow lizards of this breed have been documented. As with all chameleons, they change color depending on mood.

Meller's Chameleon

One of the largest chameleons in existence is the Meller's chameleon. It can reach 24 inches! Females are distinguished by their small dorsal crests. Depending on its mood, this chameleon can be found in brown, black, yellow, or dark green. This breed is quit popular due to its long lifespan of 12 years.

Namaqua Desert Chameleon

Namaqua chameleons are very tough and can survive very harsh conditions like those found in the desert. They tend to vary in color depending on if it's day or night. They are very quick to catch prey due to their instincts driving them to survive in the desert. Namaqua chameleons are fast crawlers since they can spread their toes wide apart.

Parson's Chameleon

This is the second largest breed of chameleon and males can reach up to 27 inches (females measure in at 19 inches)! A female can lay 50 eggs every two years. Parson's chameleons love running water and live up to sever years.

Pygmy Chameleon

Pygmy chameleons are small, only reaching three inches in length. Unlike most chameleons, Pygmy chameleons do change color to match their environment. When they are not hiding, Pygmy chameleons will transform into a darker color, resembling a dry leaf. They do this in order to blend in while sleeping. Pygmy chameleons will also change colors based on their emotions, including green, orange, brown, and black.

Finally, its tongue is longer than its body so it can easily catch smaller insects.

Veiled Chameleon

Veiled chameleons are among the most popular pets. They can change color depending on their surroundings and mood. Its natural color is green but it can match lime green or red environments. Males are distinguished by the spurs running along their legs. Male Veiled chameleons can reach a length of 24 inches while females are only about half that size. During mating, the males will exhibit compelling colors in order to attract the opposite sex.

A chameleon's ability to change color is what draws a lot of people to choosing them as pets. However, be sure to remember that all breeds of chameleons are solitary. They love their space. Providing an environment that matches their natural environment is essential if you want it to thrive.

Appendix 1

Veiled Chameleon Care Sheet

Scientific Name: Chamaeleo calyptratus

Lifespan: Four – Seven Years (Females have shorter lifespans)

Size: Veiled chameleons can get up to 18 inches long.

Handling: Grabbing a chameleon will cause it to become very stressed which leads to a considerably shorter lifespan. If you want to handle your chameleon, then let it crawl onto your finger of its own free will.

Size of Enclosure for Veiled Chameleons

It's best to use screened in enclosures for Veiled chameleons rather than glass aquariums. The reason is because a screened enclosure offers much better circulation than glass. You can use glass so long as you install fans to circulate the air. However, it's easier to just invest in a Reptarium. Having optimum ventilation will help to prevent serious respiratory infections.

Even though smaller chameleons should be kept in smaller areas, you should still go ahead and invest in an adult sized cage. You can simply decorate a small portion to accommodate the young chameleon, adding to it as the lizard grows in size. Here is the space requirements of a Veiled chameleon based on its age.

1-4 Months: 16 x 16 x 30 inches.

Older than 4 Months: 18 x 18 x 36 inches (minimum). 24 x 24 x 48 recommended.

Setup of the Enclosure

Veiled chameleons love to stay off the ground, living in trees and climbing across branches in search of food. Since it's best to set up a chameleon's cage as closely as possible to nature, you should include plants, artificial vines, foliage, and strategic branches. This gives your chameleon the appearance that it's in the wild. Trust me, it will put every branch and vine to use.

I recommend that you use fake branches and artificial vines since real ones can transmit diseases. If you opt to use real branches and plants then you must be absolutely sure to disinfect them before exposing your chameleon. You can actually use an oven to disinfect dead branches by baking them at 350 degrees. For plants, you should replant them in fresh soil.

Foliage should be spread across the enclosure so that the chameleon feels at home. He will want to be able to hide if the mood strikes.

Proper Heating and Lighting Techniques for a Veiled Chameleon

Veiled chameleons love to bask in the warmth of the sun. Since there is no sun in your home, you will have to simulate sunlight with lamps. There are two different types of lamps you will need.

UVB

The most important light is the UVB since it is designed to help chameleons form important vitamin D. It helps to ensure that the chameleon has strong bones. Without a proper light, a Veiled chameleon has a high chance of contracting Metabolic Bone Disease (MBD). I recommend a tube version of this light as opposed to the coil variety. Tube versions last longer and are much more effective.

Note that UVB bulbs must be replaced every six months. They lose effectiveness after that.

Basking Lamp

The basking lamp is the one that is used to regulating heat. Veiled chameleons love to rest under this light. This area will be the hottest in the cage. Keep in mind that a chameleon will try and get as close to the heat as possible so make sure it cannot possibly get within 12 inches, otherwise it will get burned. If you believe that the chameleon will know better than to get close enough to burn itself, then you're mistaken. Chameleons don't feel when they are being burned.

This bulb will typically need to be anywhere from 75 watts to 100 watts to ensure proper heating.

Temperature Requirements

First of all, go out and buy a digital thermometer, then install it inside of the tank. You should never try and guess the temperature because a few degrees can make a world of difference. Once you have the thermometer installed, here are the optimum temperatures for Veiled chameleons.

Daytime

Baby Veiled Chameleon

Ambient temperature: 72-75 Degrees

Basking temperature: 85-88 Degrees

Adult Veiled Chameleon

Ambient temperature: 75-80 Degrees

Basking temperature: 90-95 Degrees

Nighttime

At night, you should not need to use any lights. The goal is to drop the temperature around 10 degrees. If it gets too cold, then you might need to purchase a ceramic hcat cmittcr.

Feeding, Watering, and Humidifying your Veiled Chameleon

Veiled chameleons enjoy a wide variety of insects like crickets, hornworms, silkworms, roaches, and even those dried flies you can find in the fish food section. Some of them will even eat live plants from time to time so make sure you leave out any toxic plants if opting to include live plants within the enclosure.

Install a hygrometer inside of the habitat. You must never let the humidity drop below 50%. Increase it as needed my manually misting the cage.

Veiled chameleons prefer to lick water droplets off leaves rather than drink from a standing water source. Therefore, you should install some kind of drip system that will drop water onto leaves.

Appendix 2

Panther Chameleon Care Sheet

Panther chameleons are among the most colorful species available. They are native to Madagascar and have the ability to turn into a wide variety of different colors. Their range of colors is dependant on the area where their line originated.

Scientific Name: Furcifer Pardalis

Size: Males can reach up to 18 inches and weigh around 160 grams on average while females are generally between 10 – 14 inches and weigh around 80 grams on average.

Life expectancy: Under ideal conditions, a Panther chameleon can live up to seven years.

What Kind of Cage Should be Used to House a Panther Chameleon?

In order to make it easier on a baby Panther chameleon then it should be placed in a small area. An area of 16 x 16 x 20 is the ideal size. Once they reach adulthood then they will need an area of at least 18 x 18 x 36 inches. It's worth noting that these are the absolute minimum sizes. If you can get a bigger area for an adult then that's okay. However, if you want to keep from buying two different habitats, then you can dedicate a smaller area of an adult sized cage for your baby Panther chameleon.

Now to address the decorations. You should include nontoxic plants, branches, and artificial vines. Panther chameleons love to climb so anything that offers them the security of being off the ground is great.

Finally, screen mesh enclosures are generally a better choice than glass. While you can use a glass aquarium, it must be well ventilated so you would need to use fans to ensure fresh air is constantly pumped into a glass aquarium.

How Much Lighting Should be Used?

Panther chameleons actually need two different types of light: one for basking and another for UVB. The basking zone needs to be around 100 degrees with an ambient temperature of 75-85 degrees during the day and 65-70 degrees at night. Getting the temperature right is essential since chameleons cannot regulate their own body temperature. They depend on the environment to do it for them. Furthermore, I recommend that you install a thermometer inside of the habitat so that you are not trying to guess what the ambient temperature is.

What Kind of Substrate Should be Used?

There is varied opinion here. Some people choose to leave it bare for easy cleaning while other people use newspaper or paper towels to line the bottom. Either choice is fine. Just don't use anything that could accidentally be ingested by your chameleon like wood chips.

What Does a Panther Chameleon Eat?

First of all, all chameleons require a varied diet. While crickets tend to be a Panther Chameleon's preferred choice, you should always feed it several different types of insects. This includes Superworms, waxworms, stick bugs, grasshoppers, hornworms, dried flies, and roaches.

What is Gut Loading?

Gut loading your insects before offering them as food is important. So what is gut loading? It just means that you feed your insects nutritious foods before offering them to your chameleon. You should also dust your insects with calcium several times a week. If you gut load your insects properly, then dusting with a multivitamin only needs to be done about once a week.

How Does a Panther Chameleon Drink?

Water is the life source of all living things. This is an area where many beginners really mess up. Panther chameleons do not like to drink from a standing water source. They will actually pee and poop in standing water. Chameleons prefer to lick water droplets from leaves. That means you will need to mist the habitat several times a day. Misting has the added benefit of raising the humidity too. You can even install a drip system that provides is a constant supply of nice water droplets.

How Often Can a Panther Chameleon be Handled?

Panther chameleons like to be left alone so it should not be handled a lot. If you absolutely must handle your chameleon, then you will need to start off slowly by placing your finger in front of it. Allow the chameleon to come to you. If you are patient in your approach, your chameleon will naturally come to you.

Appendix 3

Pygmy Chameleon Care Sheet

Although chameleons are one of the most recognizable creatures to roam this planet, Pygmy chameleons are like the outcast. Not many people seem to recognize them as chameleons. They are small compared to others, ranging from 1 to 3 inches. There are several other very noticeable differences.

The first is that Pygmy chameleons are not arboreal. They like to spend much of their time close to the floor of the forest. Pygmy chameleons are brown so they blend in well with dead leaves.

Lighting for Pygmy Chameleons

There is some debate over how to properly provide lighting for a Pygmy chameleon. This debate is brought forth by the belief that since Pygmy chameleons live on the forest floor, they are not as dependant on sunlight for Vitamin D and Calcium as other chameleons. However, I could still safely hypothesize that at least some measure of sunlight still reaches them.

A lot of trial and error tests have been done with UVB lighting. There have been well documented instances of Pygmy chameleons dying within enclosures that did not provide proper UVB lighting. While that's no guarantee that the UVB was directly responsible for these deaths, it's still good practice to be safe.

Combine lighting methods by using both 2% and 5% UVB lighting. Leave the lights on for at least 9 hours a day. It's best to invest in a timer so that you can set these lights to turn on and shut off on their own.

Which Plants Should be Used for Pygmy Chameleons

Since plants make up the bulk of the enclosure, it's important that you plan then carefully. If you are planning to use live plants, then be sure that none of them are toxic to Pygmy chameleons. This is often overlooked since many people don't see chameleons as plant eaters. However, they will munch on plants from time to time. Furthermore, insects might eat those plants. Since the chameleon will eat them next, they will be consuming that same food.

I'm sure that you have already planned out where you want to place all of the plants. Wash all plants thoroughly since many plant suppliers will spray them with insecticides. You should also put them in new soil. While you do have the option of replanting these into the substrate, I recommend that you use pots so that they can easily be removed for cleaning.

Personally, I like to use a mixture of fake and real plants.

Ideal Temperatures for Pygmy Chameleons

Pygmy chameleons require ideal temperatures to survive. The first step to ensuring the best result is to install both a digital thermometer and a hygrometer into the habitat. This allows you to observe the conditions.

Average Temperature: 70 Degrees

Maximum Temperature: 75 Degrees

Minimum Temperature: 65 Degrees

Humidity: 50% - 60%

Unlike other species of chameleons, Pygmy's do not require a light for basking. That means you will only need to install a basking lamp if your home reaches below 70 degrees.

Humidity will be your greatest concern. Mist the enclosure three times a day in order to keep the humidity levels high at the desired level. Spray bottles work extremely well. Try to mist with water that does not contain chlorine. There are supplements that you can buy to remove chlorine from tap water. Most owners will simply boil the water and let it cool down.

Feeding your Pygmy Chameleon

Again, this is an area where Pygmy chameleons differ from others of their species. You see, Pygmy chameleons all have different tastes. Most tend to prefer crickets but this is not true with them all. However, their differences end at taste. All chameleons require a varied diet made up of several different foods. Some common foods are:

Crickets that are no larger that 1/4 of an inch (7mm).

Fruit Flies since they are small and do not fly.

Wax Worms that are small enough for the Pygmy chameleon to consume.

Small Hatchling Locusts are great for feeding but they will eat plants.

In order to maximize the health of your chameleon, you will need to gut load all insects before offering them as food. Crickets are easy to gut load. All you have to do is feed them carrots, broccoli, or slices of potatoes.

It will be necessary to dust insects with calcium at least once a week. There is also the option of dusting insects with multivitamins. Whatever the case, be sure not to overdo it. Since Pygmy chameleons are so small, they can overdose on calcium and vitamins.

BONUSES

Chameleon Journal

Here is a chart that you can use to keep track of your chameleon's progress. In my opinion, it's best to assign specific days of the week to administer multivitamins. That will ensure that you do not forget. Maintaining a chart is also a great method of tracking this to make sure you adapt it into your routine. It's also a good idea to photograph your chameleon so that you can easily detect any physical changes.

Day	Decication	Shed	Baby Food (fruit, veggies, etc.)	Multi-Vitamin	Calcium (Powder/Liquid)	Worms, Crickets, etc.	Other
Name:				Month:		Year:	
1							
2							
3							
4							
5							
6							
7							
8							
9							
10							
11							
12							
13							
14							
15							
16							
17							
18							
19							
20							
21							
22							
23							
24							
25							
26							
27							
28							
29							
30							
31							

Non-Toxic Plant List

Suitable for landscaping reptile and amphibian enclosures.

Choosing live plants for your chameleon's enclosure is not as simple as it might seem. The plants chosen need to be have environmental needs that match the chameleon's habitat, else they will not survive. They also need to be hardy enough to deal with the chameleon's claws, should the chameleon attempt to climb it or attempt to eat it. Most importantly, you need to choose plants that will not cause harm to the chameleon (either from ingestion or contact). The list below provides a list of non-toxic plants suitable for a chameleon's enclosure.

Suitable for landscaping reptile and amphibian enclosures:

Common Name	Scientific Name
Abelia	Abelia grandiflora
African violet	Saintpaulia ionantha
Sweet alyssum	Allyssum sp.
Asperagus fern	Asperagus setaceus plumosis
Aster	Aster sp.
Baby tears	Helxine solerirolii
Bird s nest fern	Asplenium nidus
Boston fern	Nephorlepsis exalta
Bottle bush	Callistemom
Bouganvillea	Bouhanvillea
Bridal veil	Tripogandra multiflora
Bromeliads	Aechmea; Bilbergia; Cryptanthus
Cactus, spineless	Astrophytum
Camellia	Camellia japonica
Coleus	Coleus
Corn plant	Dracaena fragrans
Creeping charlie*	Pilea nummulariifolia
Croton	Codiaeum sp.
Dracaena	Dracaena
Emerald ripple	Peperomia caperata
Eugenia	Peperomia caperata
Fuschia	Fuschia
Geranium	Pelargonium sp.
Hen and chicks succulent	Echeveria
Hibiscus	Hibiscus rosa-sinensis
Hoya	Hoya exotica
Iceplant	Mesembryanthemum crystallinum
Impatients	Impatients

Jade plant	Crassula argentea
Japanese aralia	Fatsia japonica
Jasmine	Jasminum officinale: J, grandifloum
Lavender	Lavandula officinalis
Marigold	Calendula officinalis
Monkey plant	Ruellia makoyana
Mother of peral	Graptopetalum paraguayen
Natal plum	Carissa grandiflora
Painted nettle	Coleus
Palms	Areca sp.
Pampas grass	Cortaderia selloana
Parlor palm	Chamaedorea elegans
Peperomia	Peperomia caperata
Phoenix	Phoenix roebelenii
Piggyback plant	Tolmiea menziesii
Pilea	Pilea sp.
Pink polka-dot plant	H. ypoestes sang.
Ponytail plant	Beaucarnea recurvata
Prayer plant	Maranta leuconeura
Purple passion: purple velvet	Gynura
Spider plant	Chlorophytum comosum
Staghorn fern	Platycerium bifurcatum
Swedish ivy	Plectranthus australis
Tree mallow	Lavatera assurgentiflora
Umbrella plant**	Eriogonum umbrellum
Velvet plant	Gynura aurantaca
Wandering jew	Tradescantia albiflora
Warneckii	Dracaena deremensis
Wax plant	Hoya exotica
Zebra planty	Calathea zebrina
Zinnias	Zinnia sp.

* Not to be confused with another "creeping charlie," Glecoma heteracea which is toxic

** Not to be confused with another "umbrella" plant, Schefflera actinophylla which is toxic.

Identifying, Treating, & Preventing Medical Problems

This section is designed to help you identify potential problems with the health of your chameleon. The best practice is keen observation and prevention practices.

If you happen to come across any symptoms that are not mentioned in this book (or any that concern you) then you should contact your veterinarian.

MDB (Metabolic Bone Disease)

Causes: Not enough calcium and/or UVA/UVB lighting.

Symptoms: Thickened jaw line. Thickened ankles. Bumps along spine. Brittle or misalligned bones. Tendency to fall when climbing due to lack of coordination or a weakened grip.

Treatment: Give the reptile liquid calcium on a daily basis to strengthen its bones. The dosage is directly dependant on the chameleon's weight. However, it's important to note that you cannot reverse MDB – you can only prevent it. If your chameleon has deteriorated too badly then you should take it to the vet where they may recommend a series of calcium injections.

Prevention: Prevention of MBD requires that you make sure your chameleon is getting the correct amount of UVA/UVB lighting and calcium intake. Furthermore, a chameleon also needs Vitamin D3 to absorb calcium. In order to Vitamin D to become active, it must be exposed to sunlight. That's the reason basking is so important.

Thermal Burns

Causes: The lamp is placed too close to a branch and is within reach of the chameleon.

Symptoms: This starts out as a light green patch of skin that may or may not have blisters. That area will quickly turn black and leaves a raw, exposed area that is prone to infection.

Treatment: You must seek immediate medical care because your chameleon will likely require antibiotics. A vet may also give you cream that will sooth and protect that exposed area. Make sure that you also readjust your basking light so that it does not happen again.

Prevention: Make sure that your chameleon's basking light is always at least one foot away from your chameleon. Remember that chameleons can scale walls or ceilings and hang directly under the bulb. If you see your chameleon doing this, you can use a stand to suspend the light so that it does not sit evenly with the ceiling. Be sure that no branches or vines are close to the light. A chameleon will try and get as close as possible to the light – even if it gets burnt. Chameleons do not care if they get burnt.

Egg Retention

Causes: Female chameleons will lay eggs several times a year whether they are mating or not. If you fail to provide her with the right conditions then she will not lay her eggs. Unlaid eggs will either crush her lungs or absorb all nutrients, causing her to die of malnutrition.

Symptoms: A female chameleon will stop eating when she gets ready to lay her eggs. She will keep drinking though. You will notice uneaten bugs and less fecal matter. However, the biggest sign is when she starts to scratch at the walls and ground of the habitat. She will also start spending most of her time at the bottom. When she gets weak due to eggs the chameleon will display symptoms like closed eyes, a tendancy to sleep in the floor, and will breathe with her mouth open.

Treatment: The only treatment for this condition is removal of the eggs. Hopefully, you can get her to lay them without the need for surgury. As mantioned in the previous section, you'll need a separate habitat with moist sand. After a few days, if she has not laid her eggs then a trip to the vet will be required.

Prevention: Observation! Most chameleon owners choose to keep a separate enclosure with sand at all times just in case they fail to notice the initial symptoms right away. It's better to be safe than sorry.

Mouthrot (Stomitits)

Causes: This infection is causes by bacteria that sets into a chameleon's gums or tongue. If it is not treated then it will eventually infest the jaw bone of the reptile. One fact that is often misunderstood is that mouthrot itself is not the disease – it is a secondary infection that is triggered by a systemic infection.

Symptoms: It starts out as a yellowish plaque and irregular blotches on the chameleon's gums.

Treatment: You will need to take a trip to the vet since they are able to tell you the correct treatment. Normally, the treatment involves a carefully regulated reginine of antibiotics. Broad spectrum antibiotics are normally used first. The reptile must be kept warm and well hydrated. During this recovery period, the night temperature should be kept around the same temperature as the day. Finally, you may have to hand feed and water the chameleon until it recovers.

Prevention: Study to discover why your chameleon got sick in the first place. Something our of the ordinary must have happened. Temperatures, furnishings, or even stress might have caused the infection. Whatever the cause, eliminate it so that this is not a reoccuring issue.

Hunger Strikes

Causes: Chameleons that are on a hunger strike will stop eating for an extended period of time. There are several hings that can prompt a hunger strike including a change in season and a lack of variety in its diet. You can rule out ailments like stress initially but if the problem persists then you need to consider all options.

Symptoms: Your chameleon will show no interest in eating anything in the tank with it.

Treatment: Start off by introducing your chameleon to different foods and then ensure that the lighting is correctly simulating the day/night cycle.

Prevention: Offer a wide variety of insects for your chameleon to eat and provide consistant lighting.

Dehydration

Causes: The most common cause for dehydration is the innappropriate delivery of water to the reptile.

Symptoms: The symptoms of dehydration are easy to miss until it reaches the advanced stages. It will eventuall y lead to loss of apitite, sunken eyes, and wrinkled skin. Soon after then noticable symptoms appear the chameleon will die if it's not treated. One of the earliest recognizable signs is that the chameleon will start to lick the ground for water.

Treatment: You can orally administer water for mild cases. If the condition is advanced to the easily recognizable signs then you may want to use a few methods to introduce water into the chameleon's system. This includes misting and even soaking your chameleon. If the reptile is close to death then a vet can actually inject saline solutions.

Prevention: Ensure that you change the water on a daily basis and mist the enclosure a couple of times per day.

Constipation/Impaction

Causes: The most common cause is when a chameleon ingests a solid object like a wood chip, small pebble, or an insect that is too large.

Symptoms: No fecal matter is a given. You might even notice your chameleon trying to go to the bathroom but nothing happens.

Treatment: Increase hydration and administer mineral, cod liver oil orally.

Prevention: Generally speaking, constipation in a chameleon is a sign of some other ailment such as improper diet or humidity. It can even be a sign of something much more serious like a parasite.

Respiratory Infections

Causes: Respiratory infections might be the most common ailment that all reptiles contract. The most common cause is that the environment is too cold.

Symptoms: Wheezing, gurgling, and bubbling from the mouth are all common symptoms.

Treatment: If you catch this issue early enough then you can fix it by keeping the habitat between 85-90 degrees for a few days. If it's left untreated for too long, the chameleon may contract pneumonia. At that point, a trip to the vet is necessary.

Prevention: Ensure that the habitat is kept at the correct temperature.

Tounge Disfunctions

Causes: There are so many causes for this that it's almost impossible to know for sure. Chameleons use their tongues so much that any number of issues can cause an infection – even something as minor as a cricket leg puncturing it.

Symptoms: You will start to notice your chameleon missing food on a regular basis. This is a sign that its tongue is not working properly. Also, a chameleon with a tongue infection might have trouble retracting its tongue.

Treatment: A trip to the vet is required and it should be as soon as possible. A chameleon depends on its tongue for eating and drinking so not treating a tongue infection immediately will lead to other health issues.

Prevention: Although it's impossible to completely eliminate a tongue infection, you can remove as many possibilities as possible. So ensure nothing inside of the enclosure can puncture the chameleon's tongue, properly light the enclosure, and ensure that the chameleon is properly hydrated.

Sunken Eyes

Causes: Dehydration.

Symptoms: A chameleon's eyes will appear sunken. Lateral folds in its skin will also tell you that it is dehydrated.

Treatment: Increase accessibility to water. Increase humidity. Soak the chameleon in a pedialite solution. Give it water orally for a few days.

Prevention: Ensure proper humidity and access to clean water.

Alternative Foods for your Chameleon

When your chameleon is suffering from a serious illness or an extended hunger strike, your vet might advise you to look into alternative food sources. However, I feel that I must stress that force feeding any animal is stressful to the creature because it's not natural. Although it might extend its life, you will still need to uncover the true source of the ailment.

Alternative foods should be used only as a last resort method. We will always fall short when trying to replicate nature by changing up a chameleon's diet. I'm not trying to scare you but I want you to use caution and never, under any circumstances, try this without consulting a licensed veternarian.

Force Feeding versus Manually Feeding a Chameleon

I feel that I should clarify what I personally define as force feeding versus manually feeding. Force feeding is an invasive method, meaning that nutrition is channeled directly into a chameleon. For example, using a tube to directly pump food into its stomach would be considered force feeding. Also, forcing your chameleon's mouth open and squirting food into its mouth would also be force feeding.

Realistically speaking, there is no way we can truly force a chameleon to eat. If a vet tube feeds it and it does not want to ingest, it will simply vomit the food back up. If you try and force feed it to eat a bug, it will simply spit it out.

Manually feeding a chameleon is the process of offering it an alternative food and letting it actualy obtain it on its own. For example, a chameleon that is suffering from a tongue disorder (strained muscle) then you might try to place a helpless insect near it so that it's easy for the chameleon to catch.

Some owners will offer these alternative foods to bulk up their chameleon for the winter or to add variety to its diet. I recommend that you always consult a vet before feeding your pet anything other than its basic diet. Foods other than insects do not contain the correct calcium/phosphorous ratio so that is not exactly healthy. So using alternative food sources means that you will have to go through the extra effort of providing it with liquid calcium. Furthermore, it could very well get addicted to the new foods and then refuse to eat its normal food.

Recipies

Combine the ingredients listed below to come up with a nutritional slurry for your chameleon. You can administer this concoction by using an eyedropper.

- Ensure Plus

- Pulverized dried flies

- Liquid calcium (calcium sandoz)

- Pedialite

- Baby food (high protein only)

• Carrot baby food, apple sauce (for hydration)

Method of Feeding

Place a small drop of the misture on your chameleon's mouth and then gently tug on its gullar crest. It takes time so be patient. Eventually, it will open its mouth and taste the food. With practice, you will be able to time the drops perfectly between chews.

Be absolutely sure that you do not put food down your chameleon's throat. Drop is on their mouth and let them taste and then swallow it.

Made in the USA
Columbia, SC
16 November 2021

49126478R00052